CANNABI
H(

THE SIMPLE GUIDE TO GROWING MARIJUANA INDOORS USING HYDROPONICS

BY

RINA S. GRITTON

Acknowledgements

This book could not have been written without the guidance and generosity of many people. To all of you who encouraged and stood by me, thank you.

Copyright © 2019 Rina S. Gritton

The author retains all rights. No part of this document may be reproduced or transmitted in any form or by any means, electronic or mechanical, including photocopying, recording, or by any information storage and retrieval system without permission in writing from the author. The unauthorized reproduction or distribution of this copyrighted work is illegal.

DISCLAIMER

This book is for purely informational and entertainment purposes in line with the First Amendment to the United States Constitution. This book supports no actions that may contravene the laws of the United States of America and makes no implied warranties of fitness or otherwise.

"Make the most you can of the Indian hemp seed and sow it everywhere."

– George Washington

TABLE OF CONTENTS

Introduction 7
CHAPTER ONE 12
CHAPTER TWO... 23
CHAPTER THREE.. 43
CHAPTER FOUR 71
CHAPTER FIVE.. 96
Other Books By the Author..............................106

Introduction

With the advent of legalizing the use of marijuana by quite many stated and countries around the globe, growing cannabis or personal cultivation is now a favorite pastime. Amateur and professional plant lovers are now putting their skills to the test. If you are a weed lover, you may be one of the several million individuals who may find it repugnant dealing with dregs of the society to get some grass to light up. The laws governing the buying, selling and consumption of cannabis in your locality should also be considered, but when you decide to grow your pot, you have the latitude to produce and consume your product as you wish. The joy that you get seeing your plant germinate and thrive cannot be described as they blossom into beautiful flowers right there under your protection and guidance.

Having some cannabis growing under your roof may be due to your recreational urges to light up some joint, for medicinal purposes or simply because you are a free spirit who doesn't believe the rights of any person should be trampled upon most especially when it regards this beautiful plant. The quest for knowledge about how to cultivate your garden has led you far and wide across several fields, and the information you have acquired have always come short; not consistently delivering the goods. This search has finally led you here, and I will be guiding you through the simple maze on how to effectively cultivate your private piece of heaven.

The guidelines listed out in this book will teach you on how to grow weed of high quality quite cheap and fast with great safety precautions put in place. You will have come across some of the information stated out in this book from other sources, but I can tell you that they will not achieve the same results as I will teach you.

Marijuana is quite a complex plant that connotes a million and one thoughts and ideas to us humans. This relationship that we have with this plant dates back millennia and has been used for a myriad of purposes that are as diverse as the cultures which cherish it. In this time and age, however, people are beginning to learn that marijuana poses no inherent threat to us as we have been led to believe through misinformation by the powers that be. You should not believe everything you are fed from established sources, mostly the government. Take time out of your ever busy schedule and research, make your findings of cannabis and enrich your mind with mind-blowing information that will enlighten you in no small measure. So why is such a stigma attached to this beautiful plant?

In the early 20th century, marijuana was commonly called cannabis or hemp, and the name for the plant has Spanish origins in which it was called "canamo", and the Mexican name "marijuana" became quite popular with the general populace. The name cannabis, however, dates far back to ancient times, and evidence has found it in Hebrew texts and pointers have shown it appeared in the bible. In Semitic languages, cannabis is called "kaneh-bosm" or "kannabus". "Kan" can is the hemp while "bosm" is aromatic or sweet smelling fragrance.

So now you know how the name came about, let's get started with mind-blowing information for building your garden.

CHAPTER ONE

The Useful Plant

Climate change, environmental degradation, oil spillages, spiking medical challenges for millions of people around the globe and yet cannabis remains on the prohibited list in so many places. So why is the plant forbidden in so many circles? Simple! It poses a threat to the financial gains of quite many industrial giants in the textiles, pharmaceuticals and so much more.

Medicinal Uses

For ages, cannabis and hemp have been used for quite many medications and prescriptions. It aids in having more relaxed periods of sleep, a higher quality of life, increased appetite, retentive memory and a whole lot of other human health challenges. There are over a hundred diseases or illnesses that cannabis can be prescribed for in health care facilities. The access to medicinal marijuana is fast gaining ground in a lot of states in the U.S while in quite many countries in the world, both recreational and health uses have been the norm for some years. With the increasing number of positive testimonies given by patients who have made use of cannabis products, it is almost inevitable that anyone with mild to severe cases of any health challenge will make efforts to get their hands on some marijuana products.

Tetrahydrocannabinol (THC) is an important active ingredient extracted from cannabis and has been used in the treatment of depression, anorexia nervosa, glaucoma, epilepsy, emphysema, Alzheimer's disease etc. For individuals suffering from breathing problems, migraines, pains of the thoracic region, making use of the herb has been recorded to greatly reduce the aches and bring about significant improvement in health. THC is very useful in the treatment of Alzheimer's, and its efficacy is almost twice as much when compared to other prescribed medications. Beta-caryophyllene is another strong, active component of cannabis that is used in the treatment of inflammation, severe pains and osteoporosis. Cannabinoids are of great therapeutic value in the treatment of various types of cancers and tumours. They are preferred because they don't have any deleterious effects on healthy body cells. In addition to the consumption of cannabis products, you also take in the cancer-preventing substances.

Important Uses

Clothing materials made from hemp are quite durable, last longer and they are eco-friendly in addition to been cheaper compared to other sources of textile materials. It doesn't require as many chemicals in the production process as cotton which has a serious negative environmental impact from its cultivation and processing. Hemp needs no form of compounds to aid its growth. Hemps also have better insulative properties when compared to cotton and have higher absorbent fibres.

Hemp plants make excellent papers, and the cultivation requires far less land compared to the regular wood. It has does not need as many chemicals and whitening process as does wood pulp. The amount of times that it can undergo recycling is also far more than that of wood pulp. When taken into cognizance of the environmental impact, there won't be the need to fell trees which are very important in the maintenance of a balanced ecosystem. Whereas the trees used in wood production takes years to attain maturity, hemp plants take just a season to be ready for harvesting.

The seed of the hemp plant is more densely packed with protein than the usual dairy or meat products that we consume every day. The seeds are a great source of amino acids, polyunsaturated fats, vitamins and gamma linoleic acid which is only found in breast milk of a lactating mother. This seed is the ultimate food source.

War Without Reason

Even though this plant has a multitude of amazing benefits to the human race, it is mind-boggling that a class of individuals has made it their lifelong aim to demonise and permanently put the herb in the bad spotlight. Corporations spend huge sums of money annually to dissuade the public from touching cannabis with a nine-foot pole. You wonder where such money come from? Majorly the pharmaceutical industry because a spike and sustained use of cannabis will sound the death knell for them. With more and more people taking the first step towards embracing and discovering the powers of marijuana, the stories put forward by these firms have been taking a serious bashing as they look to make a U-turn from their baseless claims.

The amount of deaths resulting from the excessive intake of alcohol per annum is over 140,000 people, and this is not part of the statistics of road accidents where it has been fingered to be the cause of crashes more than 55% of the time, and also about 70% of murders are related to alcohol intake. Smoking tobacco has caused the death of over 400,000 people and the drugs prescribed to you by your doctor is also gradually raking up vast numbers of deaths annually.

Can cannabis bring about fatal consequences? That is almost impossible as you will have to take in about 700kg of the herb under 20 minutes to attain a lethal dose. The recorded number of deaths as a result of cannabis consumption? None! The government has given the citizens loaded guns to kill themselves with while the healing herb that is perfectly safe for use has been termed illegal and out of reach of most people.

The cannabis plant is not a narcotic neither does it have any effect on your daily activities compared to alcohol. The herb elevates your mental state by bringing an increase in your view of specific problems and the environment, relaxes you, makes you more creative, and the health benefits are too numerous. Just like when you take in excess caffeinated products, you are also likely to experience an increase in your heartbeat rate, impaired short-term memory, anxiety, loss of concentration etc. This usually wears off within 3 hours so just like with any activity you engage in, moderation is the keyword.

So will you term cannabis to be a drug? A drug is merely a substance that brings about a different way of functioning of the human body. Examples of "hard" drugs are tobacco, cocaine, alcohol etc. that are harmful and very addictive. Other forms of drugs which are lower down the scale and not considered too dangerous or physically addictive are cannabis and caffeine. Any type of drug that is prescribed to you by your doctor is dangerous as it can be abused and overdosed leading to dire consequences. The media has painted cannabis to be a gateway drug, and that is an absolute falsehood! Just like with any substance, using in moderation is essential as some persons may become psychologically addicted to the herb just like a large population of the country is addicted to caffeinated products.

Our brains synthesize its form of cannabinoids which perform essential functions ranging from mood regulation to memory retention and hunger pangs. Anandamide is the pleasure cannabinoid which our body produces, and when the cannabis cannabinoids lock into the receptors, a blissful experience is created.

Ok, so smoking tobacco has been linked to the development of lung cancer in a high percentage of people who smoke, but surprisingly this does not seem to be the case for smokers of marijuana. Why you may ask. This is only because of the presence of THC which neutralises the effects of potential cancer-causing agents present in the herb. You can however bypass lighting up your joint by vaporising your weed.

No one should be prevented from cultivating and making use of marijuana. Even with the constant negative media reviews, the laws against the cultivation and use of marijuana, the herb is fast gaining traction with its positive and mind-blowing properties that just cannot be covered up by the powers that be.

CHAPTER TWO

The Rainbow Botanist

That famous leaf shape instantly identifies the plant like no other foliage or herb on the surface of the earth. The plant has a lot of identifying features mainly the leaf, or the rolled grass with smoke spiralling lazily to the sky from one end. The leaves of a cannabis plant are assumed to be the most potent part of the plant by most people with little idea about the plant. However, they have very little potent active ingredients compared to the buds which house most of the THC, CBD and other components.

The plant has the following parts; the bud, nodes, leaves, stem, branches and the main cola. The plant is also divided into sexes; the male and the female and at times, there may be a mutation resulting in a plant having different sexes on it; hermaphroditic plants. The sex of the plant is very closely related to what it is used for. For example, the male plant has minimal amounts of THC, and it is not advisable that you smoke it, but the levels of psychoactive experience that you get from its consumption is through the roof! The female plant, however, produces high levels of THC when pollination has taken place, but it severely limits the size and amounts of buds formed. A female plant that has not undergone pollination will not produce seeds, and the amount of THC it will provide will be higher compared to the other two types of sexes.

When the female plant has reached maturity, the bud will secrete resin which is fully saturated with THC. The experience that you will derive from this plant is based solely on the strain you decide to cultivate, the method of cultivation you embrace and time of harvesting. With the above narrative, you should always aim to grow a sinsemilla plant; a non-pollinated female plant to fully enjoy the benefits of the herb. You can make a complete harvest once the plant reaches maturity, this process involves making total use of the whole plant, or you can harvest partially by removing some of the buds while allowing the plant to still survive and flower again for another cycle.

The main area of concentration of the plant is the parts that have a high level of THC, CBD and other active ingredients. To someone not experienced in the fine arts, you may assume that the leaves have the powers, but you are far of the mark. Cola and buds are focused upon during harvesting while most of the other parts of the plant are discarded or used for other purposes. Once you have harvested your plant, you set about curing it. The curing process is merely a way for you to get a more refined and aesthetically pleasing product to both your palate and eyes. After this process, you can decide on which product you want to make out of the buds.

The Herb

The marijuana plant is a flowering, annual, dioecious plant and it is mean means of survival till the next season is through the production of seeds which germinate to produce new plants. The plant does not usually have the female and male parts on the same plant; the sexes are separate with the male plants producing the pollen grains and the female producing seeds once they have undergone pollination.

The independent sexes of the herb is an essential aspect of reproduction since the male plants hardly produce THC in any meaningful quantities and the sensimilla plant instead of producing seeds will dedicate all its resources towards the production of THC. So if you aim to get a plant to provide as much THC as possible, you will need to ensure that no pollination takes place. However, at times pollination does take place and all you need to do is keep the plant to produce seeds for the next planting season even though you may not get as much THC as you initially wanted.

Plant Requirements

Water

Water is essential for any living thing and in the case of cultivating marijuana at home, you can make use of your domestic water sources. It should be noted that halogenated waters containing chlorine and other water treatment chemicals can be harmful to the plant. So how do you counter this? Put the water into large containers and allow it to remain in the open, preferably under the sun for at least two hours before use to bring about evaporation of the chemicals. If the ph of the water is not also optimal for the growth of the plant, it should be adjusted.

Temperature

To grow cannabis with the best results, a temperature range of 23.5°C to 29.5°C should be maintained. Temperatures above or below this range can bring about stunted growths and a reduction in the amount of THC produced and its potency. That is the general rule, but some strains in certain extreme environments have adapted to surviving higher or lower temperatures. The indica varieties are better suited to grow optimally in the temperate regions of the world while the sativa varieties do better in the tropics.

Light

Plants require a constant supply of photosynthetically active radiation (PAR) which is absorbed by the chlorophyll in the leaves of the herb. Herbs need at least 12 hours of full daytime light and 12 hours of darkness to begin flowering. With your indoor cultivation, you need to adequately regulate the amount of light your plants get each day to get the best results.

Nutrients

The marijuana plant needs a wide array of nutrients depending on the stage of its growth.

Providing a constant and adequate supply of nutrients will ensure optimal growth and production of THC. A growing plant requires more nitrogen while an almost matured plant will take in more phosphorus.

LIFE CYCLE

The cannabis plant has six main stages in its life cycle. Listed below are the sequential steps the herb follows till it gets to maturity.

Germination

This is the stage in which the embryo within the seed bursts open to release the root and leaves. The germination process is made possible through the presence of adequate moisture and optimal temperature. The tender root pushes through into the soil and fixes the plant firmly as it rises from the ground. The two small leaves gradually open as it takes in the sunlight and jettisons the seed coat. Germination takes place within 24 hours to 10 hours if the right conditions are present. Care should be taken not to touch the seedling at this point as it is extremely fragile and may get damaged.

The Seedling

A pair of leaves with serrated edges now begins to show at this stage. This is the signature identity of the marijuana plant. The stage is usually outgrown in about a month.

Vegetative Stage

The plant grows quite fast as it takes in as much sunlight as it can take to produce a store of energy. The plant becomes stronger, grows taller, more leaves are produced, and it becomes sturdier. Do not be alarmed when some of the leaves begin to drop as it is part of the growing process. The number of leaflets available on each leaf will increase from as little as three to as much as ten to thirteen. The female plants tend to have more branches, have more leaves at the apex and are shorter when compared to the male plants.

The Pre-flowering Stage

During the season when there is an equal amount of daylight and darkness, there will be more generation of nodes on the plant which results in calyxes which eventually forms the buds on the plant. The plant increases in volume, girth and length as it reaches out to the sky. The duration lasts a maximum of two weeks.

Flowering Stage

This stage can last between two to five months as the plant begins to produce flowers. The calyxes on the female plant produce white hair-like projections called stigmas while the male plant produces tiny orange-like organelles. You will be able to differentiate the sexes of the plant about two to three weeks after the plant begins to flower.

Production of Seed

After the flowering has been completed, the male releases its pollen grains which are carried by the wind to the open female flowers where pollination can take place if it lands on stigma. The stigma on the female changes from whitish colouration to brownish until it matures and the seed is dispersed through an explosion mechanism all around. Once the seeds land on suitable surfaces, the life cycle begins all over again.

Sexing

Sexing is the termed used to determine the sex of a cannabis plant. This is only feasible when the plant is flowering. Your aim may be to get all non-pollinated female flowers so you will be quite apprehensive about having male flowers in the mix. You need to be 100% certain of the sexes of the plant before you begin to evict the "unwanted" guests.

Trichomes

These are bundles of tiny growths that cover the surface of the buds. The resin makes the bud look whitish when still growing and it gradually turns creamy in colour as the ageing process continues. The trichomes are the unique part of the plant where THC and other essential active ingredients can be found. The amount of THC a plant produces is directly correlated to the strain, method of cultivation, availability of nutrients and a host of other factors. You don't have to worry too much about the amount of THC you can get out of a plant. Your objective is to increase the potency and get a quality product.

Cannabis Varieties

Having a variety of cannabis strains is the spice of life and having just one type of beautiful plant will be a great travesty to all we weed lovers. The three major varieties are the indica, sativa and the ruderalis. The much need components that makes weed so much treasured are the THC and CBD, and these varieties have them. The THC is an ingredient in the cannabis that gives you that feeling of euphoria and highness when you consume it while the CBD, on the other hand, has a calming effect and sedates the human body. The amount of these two ingredients in the weed you consume is what is responsible for the impact it has on you. The ruderalis, on the other hand, contains a higher percentage of CBD to THC. The Ruderalis is unique in that it undergoes "auto-flowering". This is a word used to describe a flowering process that occurs irrespective of the amount of sunlight that a plant gets. Due to this unique ability, the ruderalis is genetically crossbred with other varieties to bring about an early maturation period. This crossing is only done by breeders when necessary. The main crosses done is usually between the indica and the sativa.

Active Ingredients

Cannabis contains a lot of ingredients that are of immense values to us. They are called the cannabinoids. The main ones, however, are the THC and CBD and others include, CDC, CBN, CBDV, CBL, THCV etc. The THC is responsible for the "head high". All the plants vary in the amount of THC they contain, while some may have only THCs, others may have very minimal amounts while others will have varying compositions of both THC and CBD. A high-quality plant will have significant levels of both THC and CBD. When we describe THC quantities and THC levels of a plant, it is simply a reference to how much resin containing the THC can be obtained from that plant and how potent the THC is. The THC quantities a plant produces is entirely in your hands based on how you cultivate and nurture your plants while the THC levels are entirely genetic. For example, a bud may contain about 30% THC, with a level of 5. The quantity of 30% is a variable due to the environmental conditions and will quickly change once you apply a different set of abiotic factors necessary for its growth. The THC level of 5 will, however, remain constant. It is to be noted that some plants have been modified to produce no THC at all due to regulations by the state. When cannabis is cultivated in such places, it is mainly for industrial purposes, and hemp is produced for paper, clothing materials etc. Such strains have no medicinal properties, and you won't get a high or calming effect when you make use of them.

Head in the Clouds

I believe that at this point, you should have a clear idea of what you want in a cannabis plant either for a pleasurable smoke or other uses. Your main focus is to harvest a sensimilla with vast amounts of buds, resins and high levels of THC. The cured buds should also titillate your senses with pleasing aromas. Don't get carried away with all the esoteric sensory stimulations however as you may just get knocked down flat by the potency of a plant. This is relative though as some of us will prefer to get a "head high" and still be very active and still do some stuff around us, while some other folks appreciate the sedating feelings called the "couch effect". The two major varieties of cannabis, the sativa and the indica give two very distinct different highs, and the levels of each high are as a result of the time of maturity and harvesting. When you also carry out a cross of both varieties to produce a sativa/indica or indica/Sativa strain, the quantities and levels of THC and CBD will vary.

CHAPTER THREE

The Growth Space

With the basic knowledge of cannabis out of the way, now let us proceed with the cultivation environment. This is a space where you as the cultivator will exercise your powers and skills to produce high-quality grass. Some important factors need to be carefully considered before setting up your space.

Security

Cultivation of your cannabis within an enclosed environment preferably indoors will offer a semblance of protection from animals, pests and unfavourable environmental conditions. They are all crucial factors to consider but none more than human interference. Growing and consumption of cannabis may or may not be legal in your locale, but you will need to avoid prying eyes for your convenience and privacy. These highly valuable plants readily bring about theft and the law may also come down heavy on you if the cultivation of the plant is not yet legalised in your state — so the need to grow indoors from every form of distraction that may hinder the successful advancement of your plants.

If you are suspected of growing cannabis is a state where it is forbidden, the only way the law enforcement agencies can confirm this is by actually searching your home, and a search warrant will be needed. The likelihood of you been detected is very low unlike if the plant is grown outdoors in open fields. You should be very conversant about the laws regarding the possession, growing, consumption and sale of cannabis and cannabis products in your area. This will offer you a sense and measure of protection in the case that the law comes calling. The number of indoor growers that have a brush with the law is minuscule compared to the majority of cultivators who grow their plants with peace of mind with not even the nosy neighbours ever having an inkling of what you are nurturing within the walls of your home. Do not EVER tell anyone that you are cultivating cannabis. That is the cardinal rule of marijuana growers followed closely by never selling your products unless you have the license to grow and distribute through a cannabis dispensary. If you have a huge heart and light up some weeds with your friends from time to time, never confide in them the source of the pot and make sure you never sell it to them too. If you want to grow with peace of mind, it is pertinent that you cross all your "I's" and dot your "t's".

The Growing Area

Space available for growing your weed is a prime consideration you have to tackle before venturing on with the project sufficiently. For any meaningful results, you should have at least a space of 16" long x 22" wide x 46" tall. It is entirely possible to achieve your objectives with a much lesser area, but you should always factor in the height of the plant. You may also be seriously lacking any living space due to your living conditions; which may be in an apartment block. In this case, you need to get creative with whatever little space you have at your disposal. Do you have a closet that you can do without? Then it is time for some modifications to get it in shape for some prime growing time. Here are some of the adjustments you need to make;

Electricity

Since space is enclosed and no access to light, air and other requirements essential for the growth of the plant, there is a need to provide a source of electricity to facilitate a functional system. A grounded power source that can conveniently power six to eight plugs will do just fine. You need to be cautious because you are making use of electricity in the growing area, and there is also the presence of water there. That is a very lethal combination which can have dire consequences if one becomes too lax. All plugs and wirings should be kept away from contact with water by keeping them away from the floor. The occurrence of a fire outbreak is a very real possibility if adequate care is not taken which may lead to the discovery of your cannabis, loss of property and life.

Light Control

To effectively be in charge of when your plant starts to flower, it is pertinent that the grow space be light proof; that is impervious to any light from the outside. How do you ensure this? Go into the build space, shut the door and stay there until you cannot see anything, not even your hands. If you can make out any shape, then it is evident that there is light getting into the room and you need to make adjustments. You can seal out any light from getting in by sealing all the edges with thick black plastic wrappings, black tapes or any other suitable material that will effectively do the job at hand. Since you want to be in charge of the amount of light the plant gets, you should also aim for materials used in the construction of the grow space to be light reflective; though not materials that will absorb the much-needed light, however. A pure white surface will do just fine. Do not be tempted to make use of glass panes as they will deprive the plant of the useful photosynthetic active radiation.

Ventilation

All living organisms need a constant availability of air for their survival, and your plants are not exempt. Your growing space should have tube or vent that brings in regular air supply into the enclosure and another pipe that will take out air. The arrangement should be such that the intake tube is close to the ground while the exit tube should be close to the top of the compartment. The construction should be done appropriately to prevent any light from getting in. The air ventilation tubes do not just bring and remove air; they also function in the regulation of temperature. When you put on the light in the space, the temperature will soar, and the only way to keep the environment cool is by the inflow of fresh air and the removal of hot air.

Lightning

Your lightning apparatus will set you back a few hundred bucks, and this is worth it because they are the soul of any growing operation. In time past, growers made use of high-pressure sodium lamps (HPS) or metal halide lamps (MH). These types of bulbs are not energy friendly, and the amount of heat generated needs to be removed continuously which was a significant source of plant failure if not adequately attended to. They have also been reported to case fires and plants are not spared the heat they generate as they constantly get burnt. With the coming of age of modern technology, there are now LED lamps that are more energy efficient and produce far less heat compared to the bulbs from decades ago.

With the presence of a 100-watt LED grow light, a 12 square feet area of cultivated cannabis will be sufficiently taken care of. The use of LED lights will spare you the enormous electricity bills, potential fire hazards, nosy neighbours and intrusive law enforcement agents. Make use of a timer to turn on and turn off the LED lights as required. When in the grow space, you need a source of light to work and attend to your plants as the colour given off by the LED lamp may not afford you clear vision. A small handheld touch or reading light will be sufficient, but always make sure that you switch it off whenever you are done with attending to your plants to avoid any disruptions with the lighting cycle of the plants.

Hydroponics

Deciding to grow your cannabis indoors comes with a lot of advantages and standing out is the ability to attend and monitor the progress of the plant effectively. You also decide which method of cultivation bests suits you. Here comes in the hydroponics which is a growing of plants without the use of the traditional methods of using soil. The purpose of hydroponics has resulted in a superior quality of weed as the plant has an almost never-ending of the right environmental factors, nutrients and care it needs to blossom.

The hydroponic system is much more independent compared to the use of soil, and this gives you more time on your hands to attend to other stuff. You may leave town for a few days and have no worries at all about your plant. It is a simple and clean system for discretely cultivating cannabis.

The "bubbler" system is the most friendly user hydroponic system out there now. To set up this system, you will need a reservoir of most times a bucket will suffice or any other container but black to prevent the growth of algae that will use up the nutrients meant for the plant. If space is not a challenge, then a large container which will readily allow for the easy growth of several plants can be used.

The water needs to be continually oxygenated, and this is made possible by the use of an air pump. The air tube should be submerged and kept in place using a piece of weight that will not rust, react or dissolve in the water. The container housing the hydroponic system will have a top in which suitably sized plastic wired pots filled with inert pebbles to support the plant are placed in. The plant is then finally allowed to germinate and sprout in a rockwool cube put firmly inside the rocks. The Rockwool acts as an anchor for the plants and due to its absorbent nature, serves as a medium through which the plant can absorb moisture and essential nutrients. Periodically introduce liquid nutrients into the reservoir. The net pots should be arranged firmly into the top of the container to prevent the entrance of any light. An extra hole can be left at the top of the container. This serves as a portal through which water, nutrients and other materials can be introduced into the reservoir. The hole should be plugged when not in use.

Taking into consideration that the growth medium liquid, the pH of the fluid should be checked before the cultivation starts and periodically after that to ensure it does not get too acidic or basic. The marijuana plant loves a slightly acidic or neutral environment of pH levels 5 – 6. If your plants are cultivated in any pH levels outside this range, you will have stunted plants which have been deprived of the essential nutrients needed for proper growth. Once you notice any abnormal changes in your plant, most times from colour changes in the leaves or the appearance of spots, the first point of call to determine what the problem can be is to check the pH of the water. There are easy and relatively inexpensive ways to determine the pH levels of the water. You can make use of electric testers or pH test strips. There are also other unconventional ways of adjusting the pH levels of the water by adding basic or acidic materials until the desired pH levels are attained. You should take note that all the elements ranging from nutrients, supplements etc. will effectively change the pH of the natural water. You may need to adjust the pH but sometimes; you will discover that despite all the additions to the water, it maintains levels that your plants will thrive in.

Nutrients

The nutrients needed by your plant been cultivated in the hydroponic system will vary based on the level of development because the stages of growth require varying degrees and types of nutrients. To avoid you getting confused and may be messing up the formulation and time of application of nutrients for your weed, then it is best that you make use of a full-spectrum nutrient base that will effectively cater for the needs of your cannabis plant from sprouting, flowering, maturing and harvesting. So you may be undecided about either going for organic or artificial nutrients to make use of, all you need to do is read up on cultivating tomatoes. Tomatoes and cannabis have the same nutritional requirements. When starting up the hydroponic system, add the nutrients gradually to avoid burning the plants. Do not at any point overload the system with nutrients. The plants will only absorb a fixed amount and no matter the overload you add to the system, it will go to waste and eventually harm your plants. There will be a gradual drying up and wilting of the pant from the root up to the stem and leaves. How do you avoid burning your plant with a nutrient overload? If for example the instruction on the package states three tablespoons per gallon and you have plants just beginning to germinate, you should at no point apply the three tablespoons. Most often than not, the directions on nutrient packs are for almost or fully matured plants unless otherwise stated. So in this case, apply a tenth of what is indicated on the packet. Then as the days and weeks go by, steadily increase the number of nutrients that you apply to the system. This will enable them to acclimatise to new concentration change without undergoing any sudden shocks. All it needs is constant practice and an eye for details and sudden change in the plants. As your cannabis grows and matures, it does not necessarily require the full nutrient application as directed on the package, so long as the plant is healthy and growing fine. In addition to the regular nutrient applications, ensure that you add some supplements to stimulate cell wall growth, root development and general well being of the plant. Whatever nutrient, supplement or stimulants that you are going to be using should be safe and approved for human use.

Controlling the Aroma

Cannabis has that distinct and easy to identify smell that is a big giveaway especially if you are discrete about your cultivation. No matter the stage of growth of your plant, there will be some level of odour that will emanate from them. Some folks have a very sharp sense of smell and can easily tell that you have some weed in the house while others may not be able to identify it. So what you need to do in other to prevent too many inquisitive and brush with the law is to mask the smell effectively. There are electronic devices that generate ozone which attaches to the odour substrates and destroys it. Constant use of this method is however not encouraged as it can have harmful side effects on the human respiratory system. If you have no option but to make use of it, ensure that the air is vented outside the house and never inside. You can make use of air filters that have charcoal as the main component. Charcoal is very useful in that it can also serve as a filtration agent for your household. After all, have been said and done, you may want to consider the varieties of cannabis to cultivate as the strength of the odour varies considerably. Your location will be a significant determining factor also. If you are in an isolated place, and little or no human contact, growing cannabis with a powerful odour will not pose any challenge. This cannot be said for an individual living in the city or suburbs with neighbours all around. So pick your fragrance producing plant wisely.

Pestilence

Dealing with bugs can be a headache no one wants to endure. Preventing the bugs from getting into your sanctuary rather than having to deal with them is the better way to go. It will save you costs, time and lost plants. Bugs can be quite resilience and will survive almost anything you throw at them. The moment they creep into the hold, you will have to deal with them continuously for as long as your plants manage to survive. The first step towards ensuring you don't have a bug infestation is to ensure the soil, containers and other equipment you will be using are fully sterilised; that's if you intend using soil to grow your cannabis. There is also a slight possibility of cross-contamination from other plants and animals. So always make sure you don't mistakenly bring in plants from different sources into the room, and it must also be a no pet zone.

Carry out periodic checking of the plant for any sign of bugs, eggs or any other sign of ill health. If despite all your best practices, bugs infest the sanctuary, you will have to fumigate using a purely insect-killing chemical that will not affect non-targeted organisms and you too.

You may not easily pick out the symptoms until your plants suddenly appear weak and forlorn. This is mostly caused by spider mites that produced webs and hang to the surfaces of the leaves creating holes and spots on the foliage. The leaves lose all their shine and bounce as they continue to lose vital enzymes to the mites. Locating the insects and the eggs may be a little difficult unless you make use of a magnifying glass to have a closer look at every nook and cranny of your plant. The moment you spot an insect infestation, you should take action immediately. Some of the toxic substances in the insecticides can harm man, but they often break down and become quite harmless to man in about a week. So always read the contents of the pack and directions on how to use. Constant spraying every four to five days for about twenty-one days will ensure you have an insect-free room because the eggs and adults will have been destroyed.

Growing indoors will prevent you from having to deal with a constant onslaught of pests and diseases though you are not entirely in the clear, the occurrences are reduced due to the environment you are cultivating in.

Getting Rid of Pests

If after all your efforts, the bugs and pests persist, making use of insecticides as already discussed is one way to go, but some folks will not want to make use of synthetic chemicals. You can immediately bring about auto-flowering in your plant. Matured plants with flowers are much more resistant to the attacks by pests and bugs. After all, techniques have been employed, and there is still no apparent changes, then it is advisable you make use of insecticides even if it's against your standard practice unless you want to see your loved plants wiped out. Rotenone and pyrethrum are some of the active ingredients that you should look out for in sprays. Carefully read the instructions on the can to ensure no harm comes to non-target organisms. Degradation of the chemicals occurs a few days after use so your weed is not contaminated and it is safe to consume. Before making use of the insecticide in the sanctuary, remove all in yellowing and wilting leaves, and whatever form of spraying is not to be done once your plants have begun to flower.

Pruning

The primary reason why pruning is done is to allow for an unhindered flow of sap from the roots straight to the buds where it accelerates the development of the buds. If some branches and leaves are not punned, vital fluid and energy that could have been used for bud production will be channeled to other less wanted processes. Pruning also stimulates lateral growth in plants. So if your plant at about twenty-one days is a bit thin looking with few leaves and branches, then you should prune it to stimulate the growth of more leaves. At this stage, the plant should have at least four to five leaf clusters at the top of the plant.

The pruning process involves cutting the joint where two branches meet. You can make use of a small knife. The cut off branch can then be placed in a water solution rich in nutrients or soil. This will develop into a new plant which is a perfect copy of the parent plant. You can make as many cuts from the parent as you want from the different branches as the continuous cutting will stimulate the formation of two new branches from that point of cutting.

Test Run

After you must have set up the sanctuary, there is the need to test the equipment to ensure that it is fully functional. If a hydroponic system is in place, fill the containers with water, put on the air pump, vents etc. Let it run for at least twenty-four hours then check the temperature within the enclosure; the maximum temperature should not be above 32°C. If it is above this, then adjustments need to be made. Check the vent systems to make sure warm air is continuously let out while fresh air is drawn in. All containers, materials, growth medium etc. should be fully sterilised before planting to avoid issues with pests and diseases.

CHAPTER FOUR

Seeds

You can get high-quality seeds from companies who specialize in producing high-quality cannabis seeds and products. The variety and strain of the cannabis you intend to cultivate will determine the amount of funds you will shell out. Obtaining your seeds most often than not will take some time before getting to you because the companies are not based in the US for those of you residing in the States. To avoid leaving any trace of the transaction, download the order form and fill it, put in some cash in the envelope and mail it. Do not be surprised if you get your seeds nicely concealed in some other products. If by chance the customs agent does find the seeds in the package mailed to you, have no fear as there is no hard proof that you ordered for it. There are a million and one ways you can get out of it. Most times, the seeds are destroyed, and you will get a nicely worded letter informing you of the incidence, and that will be the end of that chapter.

Seeds can also be obtained from friends who have stocks that you desire. Such seeds can be gotten almost free, and all that is needed is your discretion. Seeds can also be obtained from plants that you have specially groomed for that purpose

There are about fifty different strains of cannabis on the market all having different levels of sativa or indica. The seeds are grown with the satisfaction of the customers in mind. So whatever seeds you chose, you will be pleased with the eventual outcome. The seeds are fully described on the online portal or handbooks detailing every information that you need to know; from the genetic background, maturity time, height, odour etc.

When ordering your seeds, always ensure that you buy regular seeds and not the super expensive seeds that have been "feminised". The feminised seeds when matured produce only female seeds excluding the male genetic strains. These seeds, however, have a higher chance of growing into a plant bearing both the male and female sexual reproductive organs on the same plant. This is not a quality that any farmer looks out for because of the self-pollinating characteristics.

In the cannabis space at this present time, the number of seed types is fast approaching 500 with about 150 - 200 deserving a second thought and about 50 of these standing out.

A strain of cannabis plant can either be classified as been crossbreed or a pure strain. A pure species is the result of the crossing of two plants of the same species group while a crossbreed is the outcome of the crossing of two different species. A lot of strains on the market that I have advised you not to consider have undergone so much crossing that they have become unstable. Most of these strains are bred purely for research purposes, and their classification does not fall under the norm.

You aim to make produce high-quality products, and that can start with getting great seeds. So it's either you make use of pure strains or hybrids. Here are a few of the commonly available types;

Pure Sativa Species; this is plant type is purely composed of the sativa species but may have some trace amounts of the indica species.

Pure Indica Species; this plant species of cannabis is wholly made up of indica, but some may have little amounts of sativa.

Pure Ruderlis Species; the ruderlis is mostly a pure species, but it does have a lot of drawbacks that have made it unattractive to growers. The amount of primary cannabinoids like CBD and THC is minimal when compared to the sativa and indica species. This particular species also does not flower like other species. For example, the sativa and indica species can be controlled to begin blooming at a specific stage by altering the amount of light and darkness the plant has over some time. The ruderlis, however, will only flower when it is matured enough to do that.

Sativa/Indica; this is a species with an equal amount of both the sativa and indica species. When a Sativa and indica is crossed, there will be different levels of experiences. It is either you have a calming relaxation of your body, or you have a head high, or you have a mixture of both psychedelic experiences. However, the ratio of the species may be slightly different in the hybrid. For example, if the indica has a higher percentage in an indica/Sativa cross; you will experience a couch effect of about 60% and a highness of about 40%. If the ratio of the species were to be reversed, the percentage of what you will feel would also change.

When buying seeds for cultivation, ensure that you check for all the information that you can get about the particular seed to know if it is a pure breed or crossbred to know what properties it will deliver when fully matured.

The physical attributes of strains of cannabis will also differ. An Indica plant may grow tall because of the sativa components in it and vice versa. As you continue with your breeding program and begin to produce your seeds, you will then start to exert your influence and control over the attributes that you want to be expressed in your plants. Let us take a look at the instance of delaying the harvest period of your plant. The calming sensation that you will feel will be more while an early harvest will give you a head high. So if you aim to get a couch shock or head high, you can take advantage of the harvesting periods of the plant in addition to the genetic qualities to make the desired properties more pronounced.

Seed Sowing

If you are making use of soil for the cultivation process, it is best that you do not let your seeds go down too deep into the earth. Just placing them on the topsoil and gently covering them with some soil will ensure that once they germinate, they will go on to become strong seedlings. Some farmers prefer to make use of mounds and rows, but in countries where the cultivation and use of marijuana are outlawed, individuals have devised a means by simply scattering the seeds over an open field and hoping that some seeds will survive. This means of seed sowing ensures that you don't draw attention to yourself especially if you are practising outdoor cultivation. The random nature of the plants will not bring about any suspicion from passersby or law enforcement agents.

Germination

Using the hydroponic system, sow the seeds in at most 4/8 inch which is about 1.2 cm into the Rockwool. There is the possibility that you may want to sow two or more seeds per cube. This will give you the chance to have some plants growing in the cube is you remove an "undesirable" plant later in the future. It is advisable that you tag each cube accordingly especially if you are planting more than one type or strain in each cube. This will forestall any mix up later.

The seed should be embedded into the Rockwool, then put the rockwool into the net pots. The water in the containers should reach up and make sufficient contact with the Rockwool to ensure that the nutrients and the surrounding medium are in full contact with the germinating seed. The light should be at least about 25°C which is warm enough to stimulate growth.

Since the Rockwool is in contact with the water, it will remain moist for a while. Since you are most certainly a newbie, you may have the urge to dig up the seed to check on the process of germination. Do not do this as you will most certainly destroy the tender shoot and root system that has just begun to form. Exercise patience and you will see the tender shoots sprout within a few days. Your fears may eventually come to past if after about 10 to 12 days no sprouting is observed. At this point, you can dig carefully into the rockwool to confirm the state of the leaves.

The plant will come out of the seed and ground slowly, and the seed will eventually fall off and give room for the new leaves to blossom. If the leaves have a hard time breaking free from the seed coat, let the plant deal with it in its own as any interference from you may cause harm to the plant due to its fragile nature. Some other misdirections may occur such as the root of the plant showing up instead of the leaves. If this scenario should play out, you need to be extremely careful in making the right adjustments. Gently dig around the Rockwool and turn the plant into its right direction; setting the root system gently into the Rockwool and the leaves facing the sky. In all, handle the plant very very tenderly.

Before you start the growing process, have a diary at hand and make entries of all activities carried out, from the amount and types of nutrients introduced into the medium, time of sterilisation of the equipment etc. This action lets you keep up to date records of every activity performed in the sanctuary, and you can quickly make references to it if need be.

Mixed Planting

This is a way of ensuring that your plants do not get destroyed by pests. Planting other crops along with your cannabis is a method of biological control, and it is beneficial and will bear no threat to your plants or you. This technique is more common among grower who cultivates outdoors. When considering which plants to grow along with your marijuana plants, it is best that you make use of plants with aromas and smells that are quite distinctive, e.g. mints, spices and herbs.

For example, when you plant garlic alongside your cannabis, the smell will repel a broad spectrum of insect pests, and rodents too are not spared. Mints, on the other hand, repel beetles, flies e.t.c. And rodents will not come close to your plants also. Other plants that you can plant within the sanctuary include the marigold and geranium.

Reducing Stress

As your plant continues to grow and flourish, it will naturally grow straight up. By the time the plant is about 7 to 9 weeks old, you should introduce a low-stress training program to the cultivated crops. To begin with this program, you gently tilt the plant to a bent position and tire it with a string. The height of the plant should be almost halved, and this facilitates sunlight or LED light to touch other parts of the plant effectively. This bent or rotational growth pattern training will ensure that all parts of the plant receive adequate light and the growth of the plant will also be encouraged tremendously. When the light touches other parts of the plant, the plant will not just have a pronounced median stem, but several distributed in several parts of the plant. With this achieved, you have made sure that the production of vital cannabinoids is increased from the plant. When bending the plant, caution should be taken to ensure that the plant is not inclined to the extent that it breaks. If you mistakenly break the stem, apply some honey around it and wrap the broken stem with some bandage supported with a sturdy piece of piece of stick to support the plant.

In addition to making sure that your plant produces as much cannabinoids as possible, try as much as possible to make sure the room is well ventilated. Plants need a constant supply of fresh air from which they will extract carbon dioxide which is a necessary component for the production process. As the plant grows, the amount of water and nutrients it takes will also increase. This will result in the level of water in the container to reduce. Some growers empty the containers and refill it again. That is not necessary and may cost you time and energy. All you need to do is to continually fill the tank with water and add the required nutrients gradually to prevent burning of the plant roots and vital organs.

Cloning

When your plant is at about 10''' to 14" tall and branches have formed, a limb or two may be cut which will then be used to start a new plant. These new branches that will be cultivated are termed clones because they bear the same genetic codes and materials as the parent plant.

To cut a branch, make use of a razor blade so that it swift and the plant will not have to undergo too much distress. Cloning is a way of retaining desirable qualities in a plant without having to start from the seed stage. To free yourself from the hassle and headache of having to start all over again from seeds or cutting branches from new plants, you can have several plants that will serve as your source of new plants. It is essential that your plant does not enter the flowering stage before you cut branches for cloning. When you cut branches for cloning from an already flowering plant, the process may fail.

To clone a plant, here are some simple steps that you can follow; Pick a lower branch on the plant that already has developed nodes. Make sure that all the equipment are thoroughly sterilised. Cut 45° on the main stem and immediately dip it into cold water. Make cuts at 45° at the nodes. Gently peel away at the stem using a small knife or razor blade to show the phloem. Immerse the exposed stem into some root growth hormones. Make sure the hormone does not come in contact with any other part of the plant.

Into the Rockwool, gently push in the cut stem in an upright position. The Rockwool should be firmly holding tight to the stem. The clones should be kept moist at all times by spraying them with water and also maintaining the plants in an enclosed space using a see-through plastic. Do not expose the plant to the direct rays of the sunlight or the LED growth light.

After about a week of the cloning, the new plants should begin to grow new root systems. To confirm this, stop the misting and remove the protective dome; if the roots are in place, the plants will remove green and robust. If otherwise, the plant will begin to dry up and you should immediately revert to the protective casing and application of water sprays. If the root systems are fully formed and the plant can support itself, then you should remove the protection and stop the misting because it may be counterproductive. If you don't have root growth hormones, merely put the cut stems into black or non-transparent cups that will not allow any form of light to pass through. This method will, however, take a more extended period for the plant to form roots when compared to using the hormones.

Flowering

When your plants begin to flower, you will be able to distinguish the sexes. The male plants generally are early flowering plants s they grow faster and taller than the females. The height difference is not the only significant telltale sign that will aid you in identifying a male plant; the male also produces false buds. The male grows faster to enable it to deposit its spores from a greater height onto the females.

The females, on the other hand, will start the flowering process by the appearance of hairy whitish protrusions at the head and nodes of the plant. These are reproductive organs of the females called the pistils.

Your principal aim may be to produce a plant that gives a perfect high. If this is so, you will need to quickly identify the male plants and remove them before the fertilisation of the females begin which will lead to the formation of seeds instead of the much-needed THC. The production of the sensimilla buds is the ultimate goal of any grower as they are more powerful and all their energies are more attuned to the creation of essential cannabinoids.

Once you have identified a female plant, you may want to take cuttings and produce clones which you can use for subsequent cultivation. This will eventually lead to the total disappearance of the male sex from your sanctuary giving room for the sensimilla to flourish.

Each variety has a different flowering time and harvests it is advised that you begin to harvest before the flowering process is completed if you are to get high potent products. If your seed supply source has stated the flowering time of the plant, you will have an idea of when the plant will be ready for harvesting. For example, if the flowering time of your plant is 6 – 8 weeks, then harvest time should be 6 – 8 weeks after your plant starts the flowering process.

Force Flowering

Before you start the flowering process, it is best to have removed the males to prevent any accidental pollination from taking place. You can remove the males by cutting the stems very close to the roots as uprooting the whole plant may destroy the root systems of nearby "valuable" plants.

To force flower your plants, you will need to regulate the amount of light and darkness available. A 12-12 hour system is best. The light will be off for 12 hours and on for 12 hours. To enforce a strict compliance with the dark and light phases, it is very important that there should be no source of light at all during the dark period; not even the light from your torch for a few minutes or tiny light packets streaming in from the window will return your plants straight to the vegetative state. If your plants are being cultivated in a room with windows, make sure that you seal up the window. Do not at any time during the dark 12 hours period open the enclosure. It is best if your LED growth light is electrically timed. This is perfect control over constant opening and closing of the doors. With the controlled light in place, you will not need to go into the enclosure too frequently.

As you continue the force flowering program, the female plants will begin to fill out and produce more flowers, branches and buds which will, in essence, mean more THC. Your plants will start to blossom once there is an equal supply of both light and darkness to the plant. The distinct aroma of marijuana will begin to fill the room, and the reproductive organ of the plant will take on a more opaque colour; brown, golden, red or any other darker shade. When you notice these changes, then you can begin to harvest.

CHAPTER FIVE

Harvesting

It does not matter if you have cultivated your crops indoors or outdoors, the harvesting is the same. If your plants are grown outside on land, you may likely pull the plants and take them indoors for processing. If however, you have cultivated them indoors, you can start the processing within the confines of the sanctuary. Where the growing of marijuana is still illegal, farmers usually grow the plants in the woods far where they will not be noticed. So when the harvesting season comes, they usually go on a long trip to harvest the cannabis. This operation is not a man one show as the volume of the crops to be collected may be too much for one single individual. In all, you need to be very discrete about your comings and goings during this period and be careful about who you let onto your little pastime.

If your plants are secured away from prying eyes, the only thing you need to worry about is getting the harvesting time right. You can take some smoke from the plant to help you determine if it is matured enough to be harvested or let to age for a few more days. If you harvest way too early or too late, the potency and volume of THC may be affected. So, therefore, it takes an eye with a sense for details and experience to determine when the plant is ripe enough for harvesting.

If you aim to produce unpollinated female flowers, then the males have to go early before they mature enough to pollinate and if you want to produce seeds for the next planting session, then both the males and the females can be left to grow and matured together until they are ready to be harvested.

So your female plants have been fertilised, and the seeds have started to form, and the signs of THC production are apparent; this is the right time to harvest? Not really, because if you pull the female plants before the seeds are fully matured, they may be dormant and useless during the next session and not germinate at all. Gently open the seeds on the plants to check for the colour which is an indication of their maturity. If brown, then you are good to go.

The unpollinated female plants' flower for a more extended period with growths observed during this period. While the growths may tempt you into harvesting, you sure don't want to kill the goose that is laying the golden eggs. So you should be patient and only harvest when there is a significant reduction in the number of flowers. It is most likely that this will occur in the fifth to sixth week of the blooming period. Begin the harvest after about 5 to 7 days after the production of flowers have been observed in your sensimilla crops. The potency of the THC and other cannabinoids will be at there at this point.

Waiting longer to will bring about a degradation of the THC thereby losing its strength.

The actual process of harvesting is straightforward as all you need to do gently pull the plant from the soil if in pots or hydroponic medium before you start the processing.

Drying and Curing

After harvesting, remove the leaves from the plant and keep. They can be used for other stuff like juicing or for medicinal purposes. They contain less amount of THCs compared to the buds and the curing process can be problematic. You can clear a room and have wires hanging across the room. The plants after having been stripped of the leaves and arranged according to size can then be hung upside down. Removal of leaves around the buds ensures that the drying and curing process is fast.

Curing is done to enhance the flavours and aromas associated with the cannabis, and it needs to be done with care in other not to bring about depreciation in the amount of THC in the product. If your plant is sensimilla, you may skip the curing process. To cure, hang the plant in an airtight room with temperatures running relatively high. Once you notice a change in colour of the plant, allow in fresh air into the enclosure and gradually end the curing. The curing of the plant can take anywhere between 4 to 6 weeks. If the conditions are not ideal, your plants may become mouldy and it this point, immediately discard any plant showing signs of moulds. This happens when the temperature is not high enough. You should set up a heating system in the room to get temperatures needed for the curing.

You can also cure your plants by placing them in a box that is water sealed. You should gradually heat the tank to about 32° C. This temperature can then be increased slightly to 34°C when the green colouration of the plant begins to fade. When the plant does not have any green colour, raise the temperature of the water medium to 35°C. Keep a very close eye on the drying process so that the plant does not become too dry. This process is much faster and will be completed in about 5 to 7 days.

The drying process should ideally occur in a well-ventilated room at a temperature of about 24°C to 26°C. After the plant is thoroughly dried, then curing can take place. It is essential that you dry your product since it's a means of preservation and prevents the formation of moulds. The plants can be hung upside down, and air dry them taking about 14 to 21 days to completely dry. The downside to this technique is that some curing may also take place. To prevent your cannabis from losing its potency and the formation of any moulds, making use of faster drying techniques is advised such as microwaving, sun drying or the oven. The taste produced by a speedier drying method is usually not as refined and sweet as a regular slow drying method. You can set up a heater in a room to take care of this challenge.

Storage

Having a stash of premium buds for your use till you can replenish it will always give you rest of mind that you can blaze and get some high at any point in time. You can store your buds by placing them in an opaque glass container; not plastic and then putting it in a deep freezer. Two environmental conditions that need to be controlled to ensure that your product retains its potency for a very long time is temperature and light.

It is also advisable that you store your products separately in different containers to avoid a disaster like the formation of mould or some other unforeseen incident. Keep your products well stashed away while you make use of it for your favourite medicinal and recreational activities into the future.

Other Books By the Author

The Cannabis Cookbook Bible 3 Books in 1

Marijuana Stoner Chef Cookbook, The Healing Path with Essential CBD oil and Hemp oil 32 Delicious Cannabis infused drinks

Considering cooking with cannabis or making use of products of marijuana must have crossed your mind a few times but getting started has been an uphill task with the legal issues surrounding the use of the product. This is not an option as the ignorance, and strict hold on the availability of this plant has been eased gradually. With the regulations appearing to come to terms with the inevitability of making mainstream cannabis use, you can fully start to enjoy the amazing benefits of cannabis and its allied products.

This book is a compilation of three books; The Healing Path with Essential CBD oil and Hemp oil; The Simple Beginners Guide to Managing Anxiety Attacks, Weight Loss, Diabetes and Holistic Healing, 32 Delicious Cannabis infused drinks; Healthy marijuana appetizers, tonics, and cocktails and Marijuana Stoner Chef Cookbook A Beginners Guide to Simple, Easy and Healthy Cannabis Recipes. These books were written to start you on the path of living a healthy life free of pain and everyday discomforts, having a delicious meal with friends and family and spicing up your day.

What other reasons do you need to buy this book?

- You get a beginners idea of what cannabis is all about
- How to buy high-grade marijuana.
- Know the great health benefits you can get from the use of cannabis and CBD oil.
- Great recipes and edibles that you can make from cannabis.
- Guide on how to dose using CBD oil.
- How to maximize the effects of cannabis in your cooking.
- Preparing cannabis-infused smoothies, cocktails and beverages that can be made from cannabis.

This book is all you need to become comfortable and have a nice relation making use of cannabis. This is a plant that can be incorporated into your everyday meals. You will also learn how you can explore this plant and derive the very best it has got to offer. You have waited your whole life for this very moment. Don't let his minute slip by you. Get this book now explore the colorful world of cannabis!

32 Delicious Cannabis-Infused Drinks Healthy Marijuana Appetizers, Tonics, and Cocktails

Having a cannabis-infused cocktail is blowing hot right now and "32 Delicious Cannabis infused drinks; Healthy marijuana appetizers, tonics and cocktails" brings you the most delicious cannabis-infused drinks on planet earth. The recipes of infused drinks will start you off on a path of discovery of this excellent herb. You will learn how to decarboxylize the cannabis before you can start to use it for your drinks. With the dynamic nature of this plant, it is a no-brainer that the recipes you can cook up with it are almost inexhaustible. It is crucial that you get a grip on the foundation drinks that can be incorporated into your teas, cocktails, and smoothies. From the tinctures to the oils, once you perfected the art of getting this infused base compounds, you are on your way to becoming a master chef!

Make drinks that can be had at any time of the day; teas, smoothies or cocktails to boost your energy levels, heal you or make you relaxed from the day's activities to have a lovely night rest. The variety of ways that you can make use of the cannabis plant is endless! This book has been beautifully crafted to guide you on the steps to take in making healthy and nutritious cannabis-infused drinks. It is only natural to be skeptical and confused on how to make the best use of the bud, but with the instructions that have been laid out for you, you will undoubtedly enjoy the whole process. Have a pleasure trip through the pages finding your way through the new and fantastic world of cannabis. The drinks are healthy and wholesome that will in addition to pleasing your taste buds, will also help in some management of conditions you may have a hard time putting under check.

To enjoy your drinks and derive the added benefits of the cannabis plant today, CLICK the BUY button and enjoy every recipe today!

The Healing Path with Essential CBD oil and Hemp oil

The Simple Beginner's Guide to Managing Anxiety Attacks, Weight Loss, Diabetes and Holistic Healing

Suffering from arthritis, diabetes, severe chronic pain and a host of other debilitating ailments can limit your quality of life. The constant intake of a cocktail of medications will always leave you with horrible aftermaths that were not listed on the package of such drugs. The battering and deterioration that your internal organs undergo can only just be imagined as these medications cause more damage than good in the long run. The wholesome nature and abundant benefits that CBD oil has cannot just be overlooked. Its uses range from managing common pains and to the more complex and debilitating conditions that ravage us in this age and time. It is used for the treatment of pains, depression, irritable bowel syndrome, epilepsy and illnesses that you can never imagine will be easily handled by this compound. CBD is wholly naturally without any hint of synthetic compounds is just what you need for that immediate relief from the condition that has been keeping you down for so long. This book is a beginner guide on what CBD and

Hemp oil are, all you need to know, some of the numerous ailments that it can be used to treat, modes of preparation, how to dose on CBD and a guide of how to shop for CBD. Also addressed in this book is the nagging issues of legal barriers that are continually being surmounted with each passing day as new information on the benefits of CBD oil comes to light. Are you ready to know how you can use CBD oil to

- Boost your immune system
- Have a clearer skin
- Control those pains
- Increase your sexual appetite
- Lighten your moods
- Have a good nights rest
- Improve your learning and retention

abilities

- And have a generally healthy and wholesome lifestyle?

In this beginner's guide, you will be made aware of how CBD oil can be the best thing that ever happened to you. So for how long are you going to cope with that pain, the condition that keeps you down most of the day? Take that all critical, decisive step now, dump the medications that are not doing you any good and embrace the natural path to healing.

Get this book now!

About the Author

Rina S. Gritton has been all about healthy intake of food and living the life of a real food aficionado. With her it is about food, making us of spices, herbs, and other ingredients around in nature that ensures we all stay at the peak of our health at all times. She has been putting together great recipes and meals as a hobby and business to loved ones and clients alike. What started as a challenge to help her parents and siblings eat better turned to a full-fledged campaign and career in making use of purely organic foods and materials around us.

A dietician with several years experience in the treatment of dietary issues and business owner catering for the desires of folks to have organic and tasteful meals, she also guest writes for blogs, websites, and volunteers in cooking classes in high schools. She lives in Santa Monica, California with her husband and children.

Thank you for buying and reading this book.

Made in United States
Troutdale, OR
11/03/2023

14281621R00072